עֲשֵׂה שָׁלוֹם

There are so many kinds of peace that we want—peace between countries (so there is no war), peace between family members (so we don't fight with our little brothers all the time), and peace between friends (so we can continue to play and learn with our classmates and neighbors). There's even something called peace of mind, so we can be happy about who we are and not worry all the time. For all of these reasons, Jews pray for peace.

The עֲשֵׂה שָׁלוֹם ("make peace") prayer is said immediately after the Amidah and asks God to make peace in our lives and in our world.

The Hebrew word for peace is *shalom*; it is also the word for "hello" and "good-bye." You can see how important peace is to the Jews, because we use *shalom* to greet each other and to wish each other well when we part.

Practice reading עֲשֵׂה שָׁלוֹם aloud.

1. עֲשֵׂה שָׁלוֹם בִּמְרוֹמָיו, הוּא יַעֲשֶׂה שָׁלוֹם עָלֵינוּ,

2. וְעַל כָּל־יִשְׂרָאֵל. וְאִמְרוּ אָמֵן.

May God who makes peace in the heavens, make peace for us
and for all Israel. And say, Amen.

PRAYER DICTIONARY

עֹשֶׂה
makes

שָׁלוֹם
peace

יַעֲשֶׂה
(will) make

עָלֵינוּ
for us, on us

וְעַל
and for, and on

כָּל
all

יִשְׂרָאֵל
Israel

וְאִמְרוּ
and say

אָמֵן
Amen

NOTE THE NUMBER

In the circle above each Hebrew word write the number of the correct English meaning.

○	○	○
אָמֵן	יַעֲשֶׂה	שָׁלוֹם
○	○	○
כָּל	וְאִמְרוּ	עָלֵינוּ
○	○	○
יִשְׂרָאֵל	עֹשֶׂה	וְעַל

1. makes
2. and for
3. peace
4. Amen
5. Israel
6. (will) make
7. for us
8. all
9. and say

Many Jews come to the Western Wall to pray for peace for Israel and for all nations.

2

FAMILY WORDS

There are two sets of family (related) words in the list below.

They are:

1.	
makes	עֹשֶׂה
(will) make	יַעֲשֶׂה

2.	
for us	עָלֵינוּ
and for	וְעַל

Draw a line between the family words.

עָלֵינוּ   עֹשֶׂה

יַעֲשֶׂה   וְעַל

ROOTS

1. The root of עֹשֶׂה and יַעֲשֶׂה is עשׂה. עשׂה means "make."

    Circle the root letters in each word below.

    שֶׁעָשָׂה   יַעֲשֶׂה   עֹשֶׂה   לְמַעֲשֶׂה

    Write the root. _____ _____ _____

    This root means _____ .

2. The root of עָלֵינוּ and וְעַל is עלה. עלה means "go up."

    (Remember: Sometimes a root letter doesn't appear in a Hebrew word.)

    Circle the root letters in these words:

    וְיִתְעַלֶּה   עֲלִיָּה   עֶלְיוֹן

    Write the root. _____ _____ _____

    This root means _____ .

    Which of the words above is the honor of being called up to the Torah? _____

3

PLEASED TO MEET YOU!

In Hebrew we greet each other with the word שָׁלוֹם.

שָׁלוֹם means "hello," "goodbye," and "peace."

(שָׁלוֹם, we know, comes from the Hebrew word שָׁלֵם, which means "complete" or "perfect.")

You have learned the Hebrew word for "name": שֵׁם.

יִ at the end of a word means "my."

If you want to introduce yourself in Hebrew, you say:

שָׁלוֹם, שְׁמִי _____ .

Hello, my name is _____ .

Fill in your Hebrew and your English names on the lines above.

Now introduce yourself to a classmate!

DID YOU KNOW?

According to legend, Jerusalem—יְרוּשָׁלַיִם—the capital city of Israel, is named for peace.

Circle the root letters that mean "peace" in the word below:

יְרוּשָׁלַיִם

King David, who lived 3,000 years ago, was not allowed the honor of building the Holy Temple in יְרוּשָׁלַיִם because he was a man of war. Instead, it was his son, שְׁלֹמֹה, Solomon, who had the honor of building the Holy Temple because he brought peace and prosperity to Israel.

Circle the root letters that mean "peace" in King Solomon's name:

שְׁלֹמֹה

4

Prayer Building Blocks

עָלֵינוּ "for us"

עָלֵינוּ we know means "for us."

נוּ at the end of a word means _____ .

We ask God to make peace for _____ .

And for who else?

וְעַל כָּל יִשְׂרָאֵל means "and for all _____ ."

וְאִמְרוּ "and say"

וְאִמְרוּ means "and say."

וְ means _____ .

אִמְרוּ means _____ .

The root letters of וְאִמְרוּ are אמר.

אמר tells us that "say" is part of a word's meaning.

READING PRACTICE

Read the following sentences aloud. Circle the words with the root אמר.

1. וְאַל יֹאבַד יִשְׂרָאֵל, הָאוֹמְרִים "שְׁמַע יִשְׂרָאֵל".

2. וַיְהִי בִּנְסֹעַ הָאָרֹן וַיֹּאמֶר מֹשֶׁה.

3. בָּרוּךְ שֶׁאָמַר וְהָיָה הָעוֹלָם, בָּרוּךְ הוּא.

4. בָּרוּךְ אוֹמֵר וְעוֹשֶׂה.

5. וּבְדִבְרֵי קָדְשְׁךָ כָּתוּב לֵאמֹר.

5

FROM THE TANACH

The quest for peace—for שָׁלוֹם—has always been important to the Jewish people.
Read the following verse from the prophet Isaiah.

And they shall beat their swords into plowshares
And their spears into pruning-hooks;
Nation shall not lift up sword against nation,
Neither shall they learn war any more.

(Isaiah 2:4)

Now read the last two lines of the verse in Hebrew.

לֹא־יִשָּׂא גוֹי אֶל־גוֹי חֶרֶב
וְלֹא־יִלְמְדוּ עוֹד מִלְחָמָה:

1. Isaiah lived more than 2,500 years ago. Why are his words still important today?

_____

_____

2. List the words in the verse that are the opposite of peace.

_____

_____

3. In one sentence, describe Isaiah's ideal world.

_____

_____

The prophet Micah, who lived at around the same time as Isaiah, spoke almost the exact words in *his* wish for peace. Why do you think it is significant that the two prophets spoke almost the identical words?

_____

6

A CLOSER LOOK

עֹשֶׂה שָׁלוֹם may be said after the conclusion of the עֲמִידָה. It also appears as part of two other prayers, Grace After Meals (בִּרְכַּת הַמָּזוֹן) and the Kaddish (קַדִּישׁ). When we say עֹשֶׂה שָׁלוֹם at the end of the Kaddish and the Amidah, it is traditional to take three steps backward and to bow to the left and to the right. It is as if the person who is praying is leaving God's presence.

- -

Here is a section of בִּרְכַּת הַמָּזוֹן. Find and underline the עֹשֶׂה שָׁלוֹם prayer.

1. הָרַחֲמָן, הוּא יְזַכֵּנוּ לִימוֹת הַמָּשִׁיחַ, וּלְחַיֵּי הָעוֹלָם הַבָּא׃

2. מִגְדוֹל יְשׁוּעוֹת מַלְכּוֹ, וְעֹשֶׂה־חֶסֶד לִמְשִׁיחוֹ,

3. לְדָוִד וּלְזַרְעוֹ עַד־עוֹלָם. עֹשֶׂה שָׁלוֹם בִּמְרוֹמָיו,

4. הוּא יַעֲשֶׂה שָׁלוֹם עָלֵינוּ וְעַל־כָּל־יִשְׂרָאֵל. וְאִמְרוּ אָמֵן׃

- -

Now read this section of the קַדִּישׁ. Find and underline the עֹשֶׂה שָׁלוֹם prayer.

1. יְהֵא שְׁלָמָא רַבָּא מִן שְׁמַיָּא

2. וְחַיִּים עָלֵינוּ וְעַל־כָּל־יִשְׂרָאֵל, וְאִמְרוּ אָמֵן.

3. עֹשֶׂה שָׁלוֹם בִּמְרוֹמָיו, הוּא יַעֲשֶׂה שָׁלוֹם

4. עָלֵינוּ וְעַל־כָּל־יִשְׂרָאֵל, וְאִמְרוּ אָמֵן.

FLUENT READING

Each line below contains the Hebrew word for "peace."

Practice reading the lines. Then circle the Hebrew word for "peace" in each line.

1. הַפּוֹרֵשׂ סֻכַּת שָׁלוֹם עָלֵינוּ, וְעַל כָּל עַמּוֹ יִשְׂרָאֵל,

וְעַל יְרוּשָׁלָיִם.

2. שָׁלוֹם רָב עַל יִשְׂרָאֵל עַמְּךָ תָּשִׂים לְעוֹלָם.

3. כִּי אַתָּה הוּא מֶלֶךְ אָדוֹן, לְכָל הַשָּׁלוֹם.

4. בָּרוּךְ אַתָּה יְיָ, הַמְבָרֵךְ אֶת עַמּוֹ יִשְׂרָאֵל בַּשָּׁלוֹם.

5. וְרַחֲמִים וְחַיִּים וְשָׁלוֹם, וְכָל־טוֹב, וּמִכָּל־טוֹב לְעוֹלָם אַל־יְחַסְּרֵנוּ.

6. שָׁלוֹם עֲלֵיכֶם, מַלְאֲכֵי הַשָּׁרֵת, מַלְאֲכֵי עֶלְיוֹן.

7. שִׂים שָׁלוֹם, טוֹבָה וּבְרָכָה, חֵן וָחֶסֶד וְרַחֲמִים עָלֵינוּ

וְעַל כָּל יִשְׂרָאֵל עַמֶּךָ.

8. בָּרוּךְ אַתָּה, יְיָ אֱלֹהֵינוּ, מֶלֶךְ הָעוֹלָם, יוֹצֵר אוֹר

וּבוֹרֵא חֹשֶׁךְ עֹשֶׂה שָׁלוֹם וּבוֹרֵא אֶת הַכֹּל.